Ms. Covington,

Paint your vision on life's canvas;

— Matt C. M.

All We Have Is **NOW**

All We Have Is **NOW**

How To Create What's Missing
And Do It Now

Matthew C. Horne

Optimum Success International Publishing
Fort Washington, MD

Optimum Success International Publishing
Post Office Box 441328
Fort Washington, MD 20744-4109

Orders@matthewchorne.com

http://www.matthewchorne.com

The author of this book provides information for attaining success and living your best life possible. The provided information is based on the personal philosophy of the author. The intent of the author is to offer general information, that when applied, will aid the reader in their quest for maximizing their human potential and self-discovery. In the event that you use any of the information in this book, the author and publisher assume no responsibility for your actions.

Copyright © 2011
Matthew C. Horne, Optimum Success International Publishing

Printed in the United States of America
978-0-9794550-1-8

Dedication

I would like to dedicate this book to my late grandmother Ida Hardy whose life was exemplary of service to others. This book is also dedicated to my parents Bernard and Valerie Horne for their unending support and belief in me. A special dedication goes out to my followers and supporters; I have a voice in this industry thanks to you all. Lastly, this book is dedicated to the all-knowing, omniscient Creator who gave me every word that graces each page.

Table of Contents

Preface

All We Have Is Now is written for one purpose: to show how to create whatever is missing in your life and do it NOW. This message is birthed from observing so many people believing they are without the necessary tools to create whatever is missing in their lives. Every human being is an extension of the Creator and naturally possesses the essence and ability to create whatever is missing in any given moment. My hope is to negate the double-dutch approach to life, with countless people holding onto their dreams and desires while waiting for the perfect moment to go all in.

This is not a book for people who want to be or remain average. The groundbreaking revelations on how to create are written to elevate your consciousness to a belief that nothing is beyond your grasp if your creative power is exercised effectively. One theme permeates the pages of the book: There are no perfect moments except the ones which we create. There's a popular belief that God will do things for us as we sit back and wait in faith. How could this be if we're the only species who can consciously choose and are endowed with the ability to create? The words on the pages will bring you to oneness with the creator in you and place the responsibility of creating your life, your way, squarely on you.

The message is very spiritual because the spirit is the overwhelming essence of who we are. Any other approach to creating success can have no real substance, as it negates the true you. With this being said, we also have a natural nature that exists along with our spiritual nature. A large purpose of my message in this book is to show you how to allow your spiritual nature to dominate you, while allowing your natural nature to compliment the spirit in you. Although we were designed to have our spirit govern us, many people never come close to this way of consciousness. We have to meet people where they are. This brought about the need for me to help others to play the game of life effectively by understanding the nature of man. This is the book to introduce you to facets of yourself you never knew existed and to bridge the gap between you and whatever's missing in your life. Your moment is any time you declare it to be.

Chapter 1: The Creator Within

"If your current circumstance doesn't suit you, create a Genesis. It's within the scope of who you are to do so." —Matthew C. Horne

One day as I rode in my car, I contemplated the first verse of the best-selling book of all time, Genesis 1:1. This is a verse that I've read numerous times, and maybe you have as well. But on this particular day the verse came alive to me. I saw a deeper revelation behind these often read and repeated words. Revelation is the cornerstone of an elevated consciousness concerning anything. Anything that is concrete will continuously reveal itself to you on a deeper level if you don't place a definition on it.

The first verse of the best-selling book of all time states: "In the beginning, God created the heaven and the earth." This is what I believe to be our Creator's book, as well as His introduction to mankind. He could have introduced Himself as anything that He wanted, but He chose to introduce Himself as a creator. These are the words that rang through my head as I contemplated the verse.

Considering this is His written introduction to all of humanity, there must be an intelligent design behind why He chose to introduce Himself as a Creator. Seeing that this is the first facet of

Himself that He chose to reveal to us all, it leads me to believe that our Creator wants us to know, before anything else, He is a creator!

Verses down in the same chapter it states: "And God said, Let us make man in our image, after our likeness ..." Considering that we were created in our Creator's image and likeness, every word that our Creator speaks concerning Himself is meant to bring us to a greater awareness of who we are and the unlimited creative capacity that we possess. There was never meant to be a separation between us and God, in any way, shape or form.

If the first facet of our Creator's nature is that of being a creator, then naturally the first facet of who we are as human beings, possessing His image and likeness, must be creators as well. Our Creator never spoke an idle word and doesn't waste anything. The fact that He endowed us with His image and likeness suggests that the intention was for us to not just possess it, rather to operate in it. How do we go about doing this, you may ask. We simply create, as we've been created to do.

To view yourself as anything other than that of being a creator is to veil the unchanging essence of whom you are.

The Power of Choice

Of every species that exists, we as human beings reside at the highest tier of God's creation because of one simple element, choice. Because we innately possess our Creator's image and likeness does not mean we'll experience operating in it. The significant you is awaiting you to choose to operate in the creative essence that you are, and create as you were intended to do.

It's no coincidence that all of these verses took place in a book titled Genesis. The word "genesis" is typically associated with a new beginning. The book in the best-selling book of all time in which these verses appear leads me to believe that there is another unspoken message for us to see. Considering that Genesis can aptly be referred to as "The Book of the New Beginning," the first act which takes place in the book has true relevance to creating a new beginning. This first act is one of creation, so what this tells me is that if I want to experience a genesis, or a "new beginning," it begins with an act of creation.

Nothing in life is beyond your grasp, if you choose to exercise the creative power you've been given before creation.

Creation is at the very root of any genesis, because there is no genesis until you first create it.

How Do You Create?

Let's examine the first verse of the best-selling book of all time in further detail. "In the beginning God created the heaven and the earth." This verse is the guide to any significant creation. The earth was not created before heaven. The seen was not created before the unseen. The path to an understanding of your unseen dreams and desires will not exist before the conscious choice to bring the unseen into the seen, as this is the order of creation. You were created to bring every inner-picture of destiny your Creator gave you and bring it into the seen realm through exercising your choice to operate in the creative essence you've possessed before you ever showed up here.

The words "Let us make man in our image, after our likeness" appear before the next verse. "So God created man in his own image, in the image of God created he him …"

You existed as a thought with intent and purpose before you ever arrived in this realm. You were created to perpetuate this same cycle and bring the unseen into the seen.

The very blueprint behind your creation is the can't-fail model that will allow you to create whatever is missing in your life.

Who Are You?

Your Creator is a completely spiritual supernatural entity. There is nothing natural about Him. Since you possess His image and likeness, guess what? The overwhelming essence of who you are is spirit. Whether you choose to entertain the spirit or the natural component of yourself as your overwhelming essence is simply your choice.

In my first book, *The Universe Is Inviting You In*, the front cover displays a large blue universe that dominates almost the entire front cover. On the very bottom is a city, which represents the natural world. A very abstract bridge begins in the city and extends into the universe, which represents the supernatural realm that is our true nature. The bridge then fades because there are no limits to the supernatural, as there are no limits to you.

I will discuss how I created my first book further into this book, but I can say for sure that this was one of my first true from "no where" to "now here" creations. The cover came to me in a vision, and I didn't receive the full understanding of it until seven months after it was released. The universe dominated the cover because the supernatural is the dominant nature of whom we are. The bridge disappears into the universe because that's where our limitless ability resides, in the supernatural realm.

Life gives us many choices, and one of them is to wake up every morning and entertain the possibility of what we see ourselves being able to create, even if it transcends the bounds that we've placed upon ourselves.

Never be intimidated by the enormity that surrounds your innermost dreams and desires.

When a desire arises in your spirit that goes beyond what you naturally perceive yourself able to create, choose to weigh it against the true, supernatural you, and the impossible will become your norm.

Your quality of life will ultimately depend on where your faith resides: In the natural you with limitations and definitions, or in the true supernatural you, with an endless capacity to create what the natural mind deems as impossible? Allow your spirit to govern every decision you make. Impossible is quite normal when you choose to operate from this consciousness. I began writing a book about the universe and how we fit into the grand scheme of creation months after I graduated from college. I'd never studied the universe. I may have learned about it in brief spurts from different philosophers I studied in my collegiate English classes, but I still can't tell you how a twenty-two-year-old wrote an entire book, which is selling worldwide, about subject matter he never entertained before making a decision to sit down at a computer and trust that the words would continuously appear until the work completed itself.

Sure there were doubters telling me I was too young and that I hadn't lived enough life yet. But focusing on the possibility of the task completing itself if I lined up with the supernatural being that I was, as opposed to entertaining the self-limiting beliefs of others, is what allowed this act of creation to take place.

There is more to you than you could ever imagine. There is intelligence behind every creation, most importantly you. If you didn't possess the ability to continue the cycle of creation, which is the heartbeat and driving force behind God, you wouldn't be allowed to occupy space in His infinite universe. The choice is yours: Will you be governed by your "in the world" self, or the "not of this world, endlessly creative" self, which shares the same essence that beats your heart and wakes you up every morning? Will you take control of every fear, self-limiting belief, and negative opinion and exercise your power and dominion over it by simply creating? You can create your way out of any circumstance that you are currently facing. Live with a sense of urgency, and choose not to accept what has eluded you. Create it, and do it NOW!

The Creator Within

All We Have is NOW
A genesis transcends nothing but a declaration
That the change which has eluded you
Is no further than the act of creation

After all
This is our Creator's essence
Possessing His image and likeness
Implies we share the same blessing

The same possibility to create the unseen
The third eye of the spirit
We must be in tune with it
To a degree that's keen

When your spiritual essence
Is where your belief resides
You will make an acquaintance with the true you
And become no stranger to the meteoric rise

A life without limits is what we are meant to live
Validating bouts of frustration
When your inner-pictures of destiny
Lay dormant and not relative

It's nothing more than entertaining the possibility
With two internal conversations ever present
Never falter
Choose the voice of divinity

Yes, this voice knows where you end and begin
An infinite creative capacity you'll experience
If this voice you do befriend

Or better yet
If this voice you do embrace
You will find every ceiling removed
With every dream and desire fixated in your creative space

—Matthew C. Horne

All We Have Is Now

Notes and Insights

Notes and Insights

Chapter 2: Create It and Do It NOW

"The most significant moment that you will ever encounter is NOW!"
—Matthew C. Horne

In early January 2008, I was being interviewed by a radio show host. As the interview was coming to an end, I was asked to give advice to the listening audience concerning the new year. After a brief moment of contemplation, I realized that the new year is typically associated with a new beginning; a chance to right your wrongs and get things prioritized once and for all. My answer to the listening audience was that very few New Year's resolutions are kept, and most are broken within the first thirty days of setting them. I urged them to not wait for the new year to establish a new beginning, because their figurative "New Year" was any time they declared it to be.

As a creator, the perfect moment to create can be found in every tick of the clock. The clock never ticks backward and is always moving progressively to the next moment. Your moment is NOW! If you've been on the fence about any dream or desire, contemplate it no longer and create it.

Sometimes in life we wait for these elusive perfect moments, but in all actuality the perfect moment is waiting on us to create it.

There Is a NOW Solution to Every Problem

Growing up as a teenager, my only aspiration in life was to play Division I basketball, which represents the highest level you can play at in college. When I arrived on my high school campus for my first day, I knew this was the beginning of my journey towards the realization of this dream.

I had immediate success in my first two years on the junior varsity team. In my first year, the varsity team won the state championship, as well as the county championship my sophomore year. I began to notice a disturbing trend in the midst of this winning culture that was established my first two years: The seniors who were winning these championships came back to watch me play the next season, instead of being away at college furthering their basketball careers.

My junior year rolled around, and I began to see that my coach didn't have the best intentions towards me. I almost left to go to another school to play for another team at the beginning of my junior year, but I stuck it out for my junior season. On cue we won another county championship, but no one got signed to play at a Division I school. Division I basketball coaches love winning programs, so I couldn't figure out how these players couldn't get signed to Division I schools coming straight off of their senior year campaigns playing for a winning program.

As the last buzzer sounded signaling the end of my junior season, I knew my time at that particular high school had ended. It was a peace; it was calm. I knew that was it. Ironically enough, a coach from the school I had contemplated going to earlier in the season was leaning on the bleachers when I came out of the locker room. He gave me a ride home, and without him influencing me I gave him my word that I would transfer.

I began to get the technical process in order to get the county's approval to make this transfer work out within the confines of county legislation. At the beginning of the next school year, I was enrolled at a high school where I believed my Division I dreams could become a reality. Allow me to paint the picture: This school did not have the winning reputation of the school I previously attended. Everyone who heard about the move questioned it because of this. Fittingly, people relayed thoughts to me that I was crazy. This group consisted of people in my own household, fellow students, and faculty of the school I had left. But the seventeen-year-old me knew the importance of creating a genesis to create the change I sought.

This move was a two-step dance, and all people could see was the first move. Almost every genesis begins in your spirit, which totally contradicts the boundaries of what we can see, and extends into the realm of what the all-knowing Creator knows concerning you. A supernatural genesis more often than not begins with a step backward, the only step visible to the naked eye, which governs the thinking of most people. The second step is the supernatural move, which allows you to take a leap forward when the dance is over. It will astound every onlooker when the dance culminates, trust me!

So, here I am at a school without the winning record of the previous school I left, and no guarantee that I will get signed to play at a Division I school. But I'm all in. I gambled, put it all on "7" and let it ride! I'll fast forward to the beginning of the basketball season. A coach named Pete Strickland from Coastal Carolina University came to my first game to look at a player from the opposing team. The other team won that night by a slim margin, but I had one of the best performances of my high school career.

The game took place on a Friday night. When I returned to school that Monday, my coach called me into his office and handed me an unopened letter from the head coach of Coastal Carolina University, Pete Strickland. I had never heard of this university up until this point, and the only question I had for my coach was if this was a Division I school. My level had been set, and I refused to compromise it. He said yes. The letter stated that my performance on the court was exceptional, that my dunk late in the game to give my team the lead was impressive, and they would be actively recruiting me throughout the remainder of my senior campaign.

The recruiting game persisted throughout the remainder of my senior year in high school. Pete Strickland the spectator of the first game of my senior season and became the coach who made my Division I hoop dreams a reality by offering me a full athletic basketball scholarship to play at Coastal Carolina University.

Moments of Perfection

God's perfection is always at work, as can be seen by my story. But under a closer microscope, it's evident that the day I was on the court to be seen by my eventual college coach happened because I moved! I participated in the creation of this moment by putting myself in position through listening to the inner voice of truth that we all possess, and following its lead. God never leaves us stranded in life, so He's placed an extension of Himself in us called the spirit, which helps us to navigate through the various situations that life presents us with precision.

If one of the defining characteristics of our Creator is the ability to never fail, then His voice in you must be the infallible solution to any problem.

Omniscient and all-knowing are words which define our Creator. The solutions that He places in our spirit are derived from an omniscient perspective. The intended end our Creator has for our lives does not just happen. It takes participation on our part, or else we would have never been given the ability to choose.

When you realize that you must participate in your destiny, you'll no longer join the majority and sit on the sidelines; rather, you'll take an active role in the creation of your destiny.

The spirit does not and never will miss. The one distinction between us, human beings, and the Creator, is our respective perspectives. God has an intended end for us all. If He didn't, we would be a waste of creation. Given this truth, His most pure thought towards us is the enabling of us to reach this place of destiny. Spiritual pushes, as displayed in my story, are nudges from eternity to provide solutions to aid us in aligning with it considering the limitations on our perspective. The spirit has a place in every meaningful and worthwhile decision you will ever make in your life. It often speaks to you in the form of a solution that makes no sense to the logical mind.

Logic sees; the spirit knows.

Significant moments occur outside of your natural self and thought processes. Just because you are a spiritual being doesn't mean you have an eternal perspective. This is solely reserved for God, but His spirit in you will provide you with the tools to stay in the flow of eternity. The ending place of this dance will bring you to an end where it is evident that an all-knowing Creator was the culprit.

I do not define myself as religious, but more spiritual. I do not place limitations on who can do what spiritually and supernaturally.

The essence of creation is the ability to consciously engage yourself in bringing the unseen into the seen.

The paper of the book you are reading was an unseen thought brought to reality through an act of creation. If you are listening to this audio in your vehicle, the automobile you're in was previously a thought that someone took an active measure to create. The creators of everything around you tapped into the same supernatural force of creation that is available to us all.

All We Have Is Now

Being chosen to arrive in this realm is synonymous with possessing the ability to create. Even more, your creation took place with the hope that you would be the creator you were born to be and exercise your creative power with no limitations.

Everyone who brings into existence things we deem to be significant creations are no different than any of us. They chose to create, believed they had the power to do so, and exercised it accordingly.

It is your right to create, and never let anyone persuade you otherwise!

The Game of Life

In the game of life, the most popular role is that of the spectator. As long as you have breath in your body, the all-knowing voice of spirit will speak to you. Every breath you take occurs because your Creator sees the ability to arrive at your destiny. If this weren't the case, you would not be afforded this most precious gift of life. If you're looking for answers, look no further than your spirit. The answers to any problem, crossroads, or dilemma you face will always set before you. View the spirit as what it is: the facilitator between you and the supernatural intended end for your life.

The sidelines are no place for you when you've been created to play a more than worthwhile role in the game of life.

The spectator will rationalize the voice of spirit and downplay it as some far-out-there thought that can't possibly be them. The creator in you knows that every push from within you receive to create is directed towards you, with the intention that you will follow its lead and astound yourself and every spectator. The supernatural will always confound the natural. There are things you can create that you will not fully understand until years down the line, because of the disparity between the natural and the supernatural.

The high achiever is never afraid to create, no matter the circumstance. The Henry Fords of the world; the Donald Trumps of the world; the Barack Obamas of the world share one common thread, which is found in their ability to spiritually create significant things and events in the earth from the unseen into the seen. One question remains: What will you create?

Create It and Do It NOW

Why wait for perfect moments
When they wait for you to create them
If you refuse to take the lead
The force of creation in you is wasted

Yes, the spirit in you
Does not speak with earthly logic
But eternity in you
Does not concern itself with earthly topics

If you're circumstance doesn't suit you
Create a genesis
Opportunities willingly passed on
Create a painful reminisce

When all you had to do
Was to perform destiny's dance
Taking creative control of your destiny
While others knowingly leave it to chance

Strangely enough chance is leaving it to them
And looking for people who dance
With no choreography
Just whims

For this is the most secure dance
One could ever perform
Allowing you to create without limits
Confounding those who live by norms

Yes, you too will be thought of as crazy
But whose opinion should carry weight
Human beings with limited perspectives
Or the One who entrusted in you the ability to create

The average life is experienced
By those who contemplate
While the uncommon is reserved
For those willing to create

—Matthew C. Horne

All We Have Is Now

Notes and Insights

Notes and Insights

Chapter 3: The Genesis of You

"Always choose to hover in the lane of possibility and the impossible will become your norm." —Matthew C. Horne

I want to bring some clarification before I go any further into the book. This book is not written from a religious perspective, rather a spiritual one. I reference the Bible throughout this work because of one simple element: It's the best-selling book of all time. When you think about it, humanity has collectively voted this book as the most influential in bringing people to a higher state of consciousness. This does not indicate individual beliefs because this is a collective statement, as proven by the numbers concerning the demand and distribution of the Bible.

With that being said, I'm going to introduce the starring character of this book, Jesus, and show how His mission throughout this work was to elevate the collective consciousness of humanity, and how He disproved every limitation that we've ever or will ever place upon ourselves. His mission was to prove that with a spiritual, supernatural conscience, absolutely nothing is impossible.

My reasoning for saying this is that while on earth Jesus performed every miracle possible, including raising people from the dead and other miraculous feats such as restoring sight to the blind. Death is the greatest finality that we identify with as human beings. The biblical character Lazarus was raised from the dead by Jesus after being dead for four days. Lazarus's death is highlighted because of how long he'd been dead. The others that Jesus raised from the dead had been deceased for mere moments until being called back to life. But it was fitting with His overall mission of expanding the possibility mindset of humanity that He would raise a man from the dead whose body was well underway to decomposition. This was to make a lasting statement that impossible is nothing and that finalities are a manmade illusion when we have the power to create the change we seek.

Jesus had no selfish motives throughout the Bible, as He never took credit for the most miraculous acts known to date at the time. His concern was always mankind, and this can be found in the public nature of His miracles. Even His miracles point towards the empowerment of man and not the enormity of Him. Jesus said, "Greater works than these shall ye do." Right then and there, it is etched in stone that the empowerment in the consciousness of humanity is His greatest concern. He could have easily chosen to glory in His miracles and create a separation between Himself and mankind, but He chose to empower mankind forever with that statement.

Jesus knew the creative power that mankind possessed more than we ever will. He also knew that the most significant creations will always have a spiritual root in them. He made no secret that

All We Have Is Now

these were not acts if His natural self, rather that of His supernatural origin. The book which He stars in tells us that we have our Creator's image and likeness, the same Creator who saw fit for Jesus to visit the earth. The Bible suggests that the same Creator who saw fit for Jesus to come into existence saw fit for you to as well.

Jesus' mission was to bring us to supernatural clarity, and when He had exhausted all possible means of doing so, a large part of His work was complete. He wanted to restore your mind to a point of creative consciousness that is in line with the originating intent for your creation and show you how to create without limits.

Every natural step that He took on the earth was aimed at elevating your supernatural consciousness. He allowed man's natural eye to witness supernatural miracles to stir up the supernatural capabilities that man is endowed with before we ever show up here, evidenced in His eye-to-eye stance that He took with humanity while on earth. His mission was to simply introduce man to themselves. With the one statement ("Greater works than these shall ye do"), Jesus empowered every human being who will ever walk the earth and told you directly that He is just the genesis of you. He knew that we could surpass the miracles that He performed because if we truly grasped that we had the capability to go beyond the precedent which He represented, we could create accordingly and go beyond. He knew the importance that consciousness played in man's ability to create. Coupled with this, He knew that the same spirit that allowed Him to perform these miracles would encapsulate mankind after His exit from the earth. An elevated consciousness through these miracles coupled with the empowerment of the spirit of all Creation equates to a life without limits. Once again, who are you?

Consciousness and You

Choosing to entertain the possibility of anything is choosing to position yourself for your consciousness to get to a point where you believe any particular thing is possible. In my speeches, an important theme is simply entertaining the possibility of something long enough to the point where barriers are removed. I often tell the story of how some women met their eventual husbands.

When it comes to women marrying men they initially had no interest in, there is one commonality: although the initial interest wasn't there, the guy persisted and stuck around long enough for the woman to entertain the possibility of him to an extent for the barriers to be removed and for them to make it to the stage of exchanging vows. For a woman to make it from the stage of not even giving any thought to a guy to spending the rest of her life with him carries an explanation that must be observed. How does something this drastic take place? How do you close the gap between you and what you perceive be beyond your means?

Fear is THE BARRIER which that keeps many people grounded and unwilling to entertain the possibility of anything beyond their norms and comforts. The man achieved the impossible because although fear was an ever-present entity when pursuing something beyond himself, the willingness to move in spite of the fear is what landed him the intended prize, his wife.

We all have choices in life, and decisions pertaining to the ability to create your dreams and desires will ultimately determine the course your life will take. The power to live a life of mediocrity outside of your innermost yearnings or to live your best life possible actively pursuing and grabbing hold of what's yours is completely in your hands! All of the high achievers who are admired so greatly in society have a makeup that is no different than anyone else. The only difference is that when their spirit knew it was time and the urgency of NOW called their name, they acted and chose not to retract.

This is the only characteristic that separates any two human beings who showed up with the same creative capacity: the willingness to create in spite of any other thought that runs through their mind in regards to their dreams and visions.

Move with Power

It's human nature to place our energy into only those things that we deem as being possible. This is where entertaining the possibility of something comes into play. If you don't entertain it, then you'll never reach the experience of even contemplating it. When you contemplate it long enough, then you'll see it wasn't as far out there as it was once perceived to be. The barriers will break down one by one, and as you truly understand that the initial fears were an illusion, the power to move will take you over.

The magic happens when the willingness to move outweighs the ever present risk factor.

This is the moment of inception for your creation. Entertain the possibility!

The absolute genesis of who you are is a creator. One of the eminent battles that we face upon our birth is reconnecting to the power to create and reaching an understanding that this is what your Creator had in mind for you, as is evidenced in the fact that you showed up here with the intent that you would further perpetuate the creation process in this natural realm.

Truthfully speaking, this natural realm does not cater to creative consciousness. Life is hard, so the most prominent thought in the minds of many is surviving or reaching a level of comfort. To create is to leave the natural box and enter the realm of the limitless. Creation is an act that involves no one but you when it's all said and done. I love the act of creation because it never has to be subjected to anything or anyone else unless you choose it. Creative consciousness is something you must aggressively seek to create and maintain.

The battle to create and maintain creative consciousness takes place exclusively in the mind. Your willingness to create will not exceed your belief in your ability to do so.

The act of creation often includes the ever present risk factor. This is where the separation between natural thinking and spiritual creative consciousness takes place. Every morning when you wake up, you enter the battlefield of the mind and have the choice of what will dominate it: the ingrained belief of the world to play it safe, or the spiritual DNA of the spirit to create.

It takes a conscious effort to combat the thinking that governs this world.

You must do whatever it takes to break the mental bonds of average living that this world imposes upon you.

To dream and actually entertain the possibility of creating your innermost dreams and desires is a stretch in the society where we live. Especially with the social climate of the recession, survival is the thought that haunts many from waking to rest. With depressing statistics concerning joblessness and utter despair ravaging not just our nation but the world as a whole, there has to be an alternative to this in the forefront of your mind or else creation will never be a thought of substance.

You are your most precious commodity. The more that you understand this, the more willing you will be to invest in your mind and spirit. The mind is key because the mind represents the natural nature that man possesses. The spirit is key because if you can formulate a strong enough belief in your mind, this gives you access to limitless endlessly abundant creative space of the spirit.

I will end this chapter by giving you three strategies to remove any barriers separating you from a creative consciousness of possibility and show you how to reach a place where creating is the norm and surviving and not tapping into your limitless potential is an afterthought.

Number 1: Find successful people and see what the underlying causes were for their success.

In essence, what's their story? These people can be in your field of endeavor or anyone who broke the bonds of security and created their way to an uncommon life. I say it can be either because all we're fighting for is to get your mind to a place of possibility when it comes to your dreams and desires to create what's been missing and do it NOW!

What you will find are common threads amongst the experiences of these high achievers—similar philosophies that facilitated their rise to uncommon creation. This strategy is meant to destroy thoughts of "It couldn't be me," as you observe that these people breathe the same air as you, may have similar backgrounds, but simply chose to create in spite of any opposition they faced along the way, internal and external. Once you grasp this, possibility will begin to make its way into your consciousness until your consciousness matches the uncommon desire to create inside of you. Your spirit will recognize that the same magic available to them is available to you as well, as your being begins to be encompassed by thoughts of creation.

Number 2: Bombard your mind with messages of possibility.

It never hurts to actively and aggressively undertake self-development.

Self-development creates an uncommon story in your mind to match the uncommon dream in you.

Just as you are doing now, seek out sound messages of motivation and inspiration and listen to them often. They are a place of refuge from the natural limiting thinking that permeates the air of this world. Place value on the messages you allow to access you.

Any message you take in is absorbed, and whatever message is taken in more is ultimately the one that wins and dominates your consciousness.

A possibility mindset encourages a life without limits. It's a real detriment if you don't absorb these kinds of messages, because the default message of the world will become the default message of your mind. You didn't pick up this book to remain average in any way; take this strategy to heart.

Number 3: Educate yourself.

A remarkable thing in life is that when we arrive at a place where something that was once far out there loses its elusive luster and stares us in the face, we believe we can have and create it. At the onset of a dream or act of creation, there is always a barrier of fear and uncertainty, as we are human beings. Anything you can do to close the gap mentally is an asset to the creator in you. When we take the time to educate ourselves about any particular thing, we naturally begin to see that nothing is as far out as we perceive it to be. The only thing that keeps us from pursuing and creating in life is a fear of the inner workings of a particular thing. Once the creative intricacies behind something are learned, often there is no room for fear because we are no longer ignorant. We become consciously willing to create the genesis of anything that has eluded us.

The Genesis of You

Living from a spiritual consciousness
Will prove that nothing is impossible
When you adopt this way of thinking
Impossible turn to probable

With the greatest finality, death
Openly being defeated
Oh, your creative capacity and reserves
Can never be depleted

With the greatest to ever walk the earth
Telling you He is just your genesis
See creative inhibitions for what they are
An unworthy nemesis

When I speak of your genesis
It refers to your originating intent
Which will never change
So your perspective must change to it

Understanding your Creator
Is nothing more than understanding yourself
And understanding the blueprints of you
Aptly playing the hand you were dealt

With miracles being
Just the tip of our creative iceberg
Then dismissing the ability to create anything
Proves to be absurd

Always entertain the possibility
The odds you will defy
As every particular unfolds on your path
You'll see the Universe comply

—Matthew C. Horne

Notes and Insights

Chapter 4: Living Your Truth;
Finding Your Way; Revealing Your Light

"'The Way' to achieving your dreams is not obligated to appear until you commit to living your truth." —Matthew C. Horne

As human beings we innately possess the desire to go higher than our current state. The essence of what we were created to do is to not just create, but to evolve as well.

Evolution occurs when we step outside of the box of our accomplishments and failures and realize that there's no time like the present to create the burning desire of NOW, whatever it may be.

Living Your Truth

There will always be a burning desire of NOW, because something has to get us up and moving towards the inner pictures of destiny we're all created to create. Burning dreams and desires, when pursued, lead to the evolution of you. Creation is always present inside of us and speaks to us with the voice of "the urgency of now," which seeks our active participation for creation to express itself through us. When the gentle nudges from your spirit let you know that it's time to create, it's exactly just that: time to create.

This nudge is letting you know that every provision you need to achieve your dreams and create whatever's missing is already set in motion, but experiencing it resides in the realm of choice. Yes, my belief is that a Creator epitomized by the words "Alpha" and "Omega" suggests that there is a beginning and end perspective to your life that must have been established before you ever showed up here in the spirit realm. But considering that we have two natures, natural and spiritual, it takes natural movement to enter the supernatural flow of the spirit, where all significant creation takes place.

If life were an effortless spiritual ride with no need for us to participate in the creation of our destiny, then our natural nature could never exist; since it does, natural steps must be taken in any creation process.

To bring clarity to these statements I'm going to discuss how I wrote and published my first book from literal "thin air." I mention my first book throughout this work because of it was a significant creation when how it all came together is examined. My stories are personal in nature because they hold an unequivocal reality that can't be rivaled considering the process took place through my lenses and no one else's. This gives me more clarity and adds a deeper element of truth as I convey my findings to you.

All We Have Is Now

In my last semester of college I was offered and signed a book contract to publish a motivational book alongside thirteen other motivational speakers titled *A Massive Dose of Motivation*. It was a good start considering that I hadn't graduated college yet, and established motivational speakers had enough faith in my ideas to offer me a contract to appear beside them.

Success isn't the spooky thing so many make it out to be. When you function in the space you were created to occupy, the signs and markers will be evident. Your Creator knows that validation on things you've set out to create will keep you in a creative state with the reality that this is not just another endeavor, rather undeniable truth, evidenced in the alignments around you.

The book, *A Massive Dose of Motivation*, was written in chapters, with each author having a set number of pages to convey their ideals and philosophies on success. The response from my chapter in the book was overwhelming, and let me know I was in the right space. Many people began to tell me they couldn't wait to read a book that was written exclusively by me, and unbeknownst to them "the urgency of NOW" was already working that out. By the time the various readers were reading that book, I was well on my way to completing my solo project, *The Universe Is Inviting You In*.

The co-authorship book was relatively easy considering that all I was asked to do was provide an edited chapter and a few minor particulars and the publishers would handle the major work of production. I learned a little bit throughout the process but not nearly enough to write and publish my own book. This is where I can confidently say that even when you don't hold every answer pertaining to the "how" and "when" surrounding the creation of something, "the way" has a magical way of appearing on cue to aid you in the creation of a dream.

Finding Your Way

Before I knew it, I was finished writing the book. This was the easy part considering that writing comes naturally to me. The next phase was publishing, of which my knowledge was limited at best. But oddly enough, I didn't complete the project; the project completed itself in ways that I still don't have an explanation for to this day. I was barely living income-wise and was just a year out of college. Somehow I managed to publish a book without borrowing any money and going into debt. Every piece of information I needed to publish the book found its way to me precisely on schedule. These events took place because I didn't need to know all of the answers before I began the creation process. When I knew the time was NOW, I moved without hesitation and created as I was created to do.

The end-of-the-day truth is that God placed a burning desire inside of me to write this book, just as you possess desires to create various things as well. I leaned more to possibility even though inability lurked in the back of my mind and through other's negative opinions. I stayed the course of creation, with limited visibility as to what my next step would be. Creation ultimately expressed itself through me, just as it wants to do through you.

I still can't add up where the money came from; how I precisely was led to the right editors and designers who were capable of putting my book in a worldwide light.

The particulars of the universe and its' divine orchestration can be defined in two words: "The Way." "The Way" is awaiting you to consciously commit to creating your dreams and it will appear.

Once it does, its momentum will bring you to the finish line of destiny. "The Way" is the supernatural force of divine orchestration that ensures the divine dreams and desires you possess are created as they were intended to be.

Revealing Your Light

Divine Creation always has light. When I receive emails from readers spanning the globe I know that this act of creation was supernatural. The "urgency of NOW" nudges you to create because it sees the light that surrounds your creation. Light will surround your creation and bring light, in some way, shape or form, to those who come in contact with your creation. This is the ultimate intention of it, to serve as a reflection of your Creator, who is uninhibited light and enlightenment.

There is light inside of you, which is revealed through the things you've been created to create. Do not interfere with this most precious flow of creation by entertaining thoughts of, "How will this ever happen?" or "Am I really capable of such a thing?"

I used my story because of one bottom line: I was twenty-two years old when I began writing my book and it was delivered from the printer five days before my twenty-fourth birthday. These are not narcissistic statements, but ones that prove that the guiding force of Creation doesn't respect your natural shortcomings when you have a supernatural capacity and mission to create every inner picture of destiny that nudges you to express itself through you. The super will always take precedence over the natural if you allow it. Yes, the natural part of you is real, but the spirit is the essence of who you are.

Lean to your natural mind and get stuck in the frustrating realm contemplating what you should create instead of creating; lean to your spiritual essence and creating things from the clear blue sky will become the equivalent of a leisurely walk, as you experience the effortless flow of creative energy. You have brilliance, genius, and greatness. Believe and create.

Living Your Truth; Finding Your Way; Revealing Your Light

We all have truths
Which speak with the urgency of NOW
Of which "the way" will be revealed
When our concern is not the "when" or the "how"

Creating the truths
That you see so vividly
Is positioning the universe
To create this imagery

Trusting "the way"
To appear precisely on schedule
Is trusting the Creator of your desires
And resisting the urge to become disheveled

It may be the eleventh hour
When your perfection unfolds
But you must never relinquish creative endeavors
Because onlookers are waiting to behold

The splendor
Of yet another supernatural creation
Bringing their consciousness to possibility
No more doubt, simply elation

This is where your light is revealed
As logic cannot wrap itself around
The gift you delivered to this world
So decoratively adorned and crowned

As it is unveiled
Its light is evident
As this only came through you
To remind all who encounter of heavenly precedent

—Matthew C. Horne

Notes and Insights

Notes and Insights

Chapter 5: The Creative Space

"The magic happens when we become clear on what we'd like to create, and then create the environment and space for it to happen." — Matthew C. Horne

In writing my first book, I understood why writers often get away from everything in order to complete their projects. The uninhibited flow of creative energy that is experienced comes to life when no distractions are present. It was a struggle to create and maintain the necessary physical and mental space to complete my project, but I somehow managed to create it.

Creative space is not relegated to just writing; every dream and endeavor has a space that is necessary for it to become a reality. The beautiful thing about this empowerment tool of choice we've been given is that we have to choose to create the space before we create the dream. Environment aids in the cultivation of every seed of greatness you possess.

Michael Jordan admitted during his career that he was privileged to play in the NBA because there were better ballplayers than him and his teammates in the playgrounds across the nation. This had to be true coming from arguably the greatest player to have ever laced them up. What was the difference between these great talents we never heard of and him and his teammates who ultimately made it to the bright lights? The willingness to place themselves in an environment where their dreams could become a reality.

The Creative Mentality

The average person in society cannot relate to creating because of the security mindset that governs this world.

> *The creator has an entirely different mindset than most and is very often misunderstood because of their risk-taking mentality, which perplexes the mind of someone who chooses not to live in the creative essence.*

We are all one. These words are not meant to create an "us vs. them" mentality. But at the onset of any creative process, one important lesson is to know that people, especially those closest to you, will not understand the willingness to create from the clear blue sky because their feet are planted on the pavement, and so are their minds.

The many times you experience genesis in life lead to an evolution and redefining of who you are when you choose to create the burning desires that destiny places within you. Most people fear change, and when it's staring them in the face in the form of you,

All We Have Is Now

the one who chose to explore their limitless possibilities, often the response is rejection in some form.

"Change" is one of the most difficult choices and most empowering all in the same breath.

Considering it is the cornerstone of your evolution, it must be viewed as necessary.

One of the most difficult tasks upon recollection of the writing and publishing of my book was the mental space it took to stay in the flow of creation. The flow of creation is nothing more than remaining still and quiet enough for your spirit to communicate the instructions of creation long enough to complete the task. Mental space is something for which you'll find yourself battling, if you truly value the creation of your inner pictures and understand the importance that mental clarity plays in creation. Whatever the distracting "noise" is around you, it must be silenced, as the spirit originates and dwells in peace.

Between negative dissuading opinions concerning my age and ability to complete a book, I had to create the environment necessary to complete the task. Once you begin to create, you'll notice your spirit will become alive and lead you into still thoughts and environments to aid in whatever creation lurks in your spirit.

The Mental Space

Self-development was the first priority every morning during the creation of my book. It took my mind to a place of possibility and also served me by providing a story in my mind that was totally contrary to the fears others attempted to impose upon me and even the subtle voices of doubt within. It's important to take the beginning of the day to set the precedent of spiritual flow and messages that encourage creation and dispel the detriments to it.

The willingness to create will never exceed the mental picture of your ability to do so. Always choose to hover in the lane of possibility and the impossible will become your norm.

When you choose to reside on a higher plane of consciousness, your thoughts will remain there.

The spirit is limitless, so bringing your mind to the realm of the limitless encourages the limitless flow of the spirit in your creation.

The spirit flows when the atmosphere is provided for the flow. Let's examine the starring character of the best-selling book of all time once again. Jesus, in my opinion, was the greatest man to have ever walked the earth when I examine how His legacy is the greatest we've ever known to date. He was uninhibited spiritual energy and flow. An eminent mission was to bring the minds of humanity to a spiritual awareness of themselves and their unending creative potential so we could create without limits as we were created to do. Everywhere His feet trod, this was His burning desire: to help humanity gain a more enlightened true perspective of who they really are.

With this being the reality of His mission, even He could not help everyone reach this awareness. Many times He was ready and willing to do whatever it took to raise the spiritual awareness of the people around them, but He couldn't because of the spiritual climate not matching what He was willing to create in that very moment. Many phrases like, "He departed because they received Him not," appear in the Bible. These phrases appear because the end-of-the-day reality is that the creation of anything is a spiritual process and your mental space and environment will determine whether you get to experience the spiritual flow of creation. The spirit is always looking for a match; will you provide it?

The Physical Space

The physical space of creation is the common-sense aspect of creation. The right physical environment will complement the mental space of creation and keep you in the flow of creation. My high school dream was to play Division I basketball. I entertained the possibility of it, thus creating the mental space for this act of creation to occur, but I also placed myself in an environment where this dream could become a reality. The mental space of me entertaining the possibility of playing Division I basketball coupled with the willingness to place myself in an environment where this could become a reality is what led to the creation of it and me ultimately playing at the Division I level.

Where Is Your Magic?

At this stage of my career I not only speak, write, and publish books. I also train other motivational speakers on how to be cutting edge and enter the self-development industry at an unprecedented level. One of my core philosophies is to go where the "magic" is. This story will bring life into these words.

In mid 2007, I heard that the motivational speaker legend Les Brown was coming to my home town of Prince George's County, Maryland, to speak at a church that was minutes away from my house. I checked out his website, which I had never really done, and saw this on his speaking calendar. In addition to this, my sister called to let me know that he was coming to town. Being a young author about to release my first book, I saw this as a golden opportunity to have one of the top five speakers in the world read my book and possibly comment on it.

The day for Les Brown to visit Prince George's County arrived, and I had a book signing for my co-authorship book in downtown D.C. just before the start of his presentation. As soon as my signing was over, I drove over to the church where Les Brown was speaking and heard a masterful presentation from the legend himself. In a large lobby area in the church, there was Les Brown, whom I'd met about a year earlier. I reintroduced myself and informed him that I had completed a book and would love for him to take a look at it and write a few words if the manuscript was to his liking. I came prepared that day. As soon as I got the okay from his staff for him to review my book, I went to my car to retrieve my unedited book and handed it over to his staff.

About a month's time had elapsed and I didn't hear anything back from him. I figured I gave it a shot, but maybe it wouldn't work out. Just as I had my book edited and sent to the printer, I received an email from a member of his staff letting me know that Les Brown enjoyed the book and that he was giving me permission to use the testimonial he had written expressing this. These are the words he wrote about my book: "The Universe Is Inviting You In is a great tool on the road to your destiny. Each of us must choose our path and utilize the knowledge and wisdom that is guiding our journey from within, giving us the power to live our dreams." – Les Brown (The Motivator).

You never know the extent of the magic that is waiting for you when you consciously place yourself in environments to experience it.

Environments of like-minded people create a spiritual energy to experience real magic.

All you need is a break when it comes to your dream.

If you have the courage and audacity to create your inner pictures of destiny, don't think the universe won't compensate and connect you to things that aid in the explosion of your dream.

Understand the environment that caters to this; place yourself there and experience the touch of the universe's wand.

Never downplay the voice of spirit. Spirit knows all. So when you feel a nudge leading you to a particular place, be there. As seen in this story, the gentle nudges were evident and led me to be at a place where Les Brown was speaking. I had no clue what would happen, but I was smart enough to realize this wasn't going to be an ordinary moment. Spirit wants nothing but the extraordinary life for you. Heed its voice; create the environment and experience the real magic of your dream. It's possible!

The Creative Space

The creative space
Of which elements are mental and physical
Undoubtedly have to be established
For your desires to reach the pinnacle

On display
At an onlooker's glance
The culprit; the necessary environment
Not what many believe in, "chance"

The creative space
Does not magically appear
As you make some things distant
And bring others near

At your possibility story
Yes, some people may be offended
As it is fixated
And never open ended

Don't worry
As clearly as you do
They were never meant to see it
Your manifested images relay undeniable truth

And then they understand
Why at times you needed your space
As the "how" unfolds
Their desires they now embrace

So create your environment
And your spirit will speak to you
To show you how to create
The intricate blueprints of you

As you are still
The voice of truth will whisper
Heeding her instructions
You'll experience her splendor

—Matthew C. Horne

Notes and Insights

Notes and Insights

Chapter 6: Outward Appearance and Success

"In this visually saturated society, it's the 'upfront' game that furthers any conversation." —Matthew C. Horne

Although the essence of my message is spiritual, it is my desire to empower you to function in this natural world. The reality is that you don't have a face-to-face encounter with God every day, so there must be an in-depth understanding of the nature of man because this is who you deal with on a daily basis. People are doors and you can be as spiritually aware and gifted as you'd like, but ultimately you have to learn to play the game of life.

The biblical offering, "Man looks on the outward appearance, but God looks at the heart," is saying more than most people realize. These words suggest that although man's originating nature is spiritual, most never reach this realm of actualization so they are governed by what they see. I believe these words were written to help us understand how to effectively play the game of life.

Things get done through people in the realm of the earth. There's no getting around that. Your Creator possesses the ability to rearrange anything in your favor at any given moment, but in the same breath you must learn how to effectively cater to the dominating sensory elements by which man is governed.

Man's Sensory Aspect

Every dream and endeavor has an allure, a spirit, and a swagger.

People judge you by these sensory elements when making an initial assessment of you. I'm just the messenger. These are the rules of the game, period! I'm encouraging you to not just dive headfirst into your dreams, but learn how to project the image of it before you take the steps to create it.

In playing the game of basketball my entire life, I realized that there were always levels within the game. There was junior varsity and varsity in high school and three different divisions at the collegiate level. So, the ingrained awareness of levels is something that was evident at an early age. Even my Boys & Girls Club had an A and B team. Levels are real in our society in whatever you do.

My suggestion is to become clear on what you'd like to create and spy out the land to understand the different levels that exist in your field of endeavor. Be honest with yourself; go to where the major players gather and see them on their various stages. Do whatever research is necessary for you to understand your dream inside and out and honestly assess on what level you believe you belong. Honesty is the key in this, as this will assure you make a graceful entrance into the party.

Once your level is established, observe the people on your respective level and absorb their habits—their way of appearance and the overall aura of how they conduct themselves in all aspects of life. I didn't approach Les Brown looking like another young guy off the street, even though many of my generational counterparts still adopted this as their way of dress no matter where they went. I believed myself, considering my philosophies and talents, to be amongst the elites of the self-development industry. I found out they all wore suits, were well manicured at all times, and had an appearance that reflected success without them saying a word.

Given these realities I made this my level and adopted these traits so that people in my industry would think the absolute best thoughts concerning my ability before I said one word. Once again: these are not my rules, rather those of the society we live and function in on a daily basis. Even until this day, people want to do business with me based on my appearance alone. When I actually open my mouth and deliver, it's just the icing on the cake.

In an ideal world, people would judge you based on your talent, and the whole "up front" aspect of it all would have far less relevance than it does.

Notice I said "ideal." Understanding the rules of the societal outward game will advance you further at the onset of your dream pursuit as well as throughout it.

Please don't be offended by these next statements. I also observed that all of the "big time" motivational speakers were driving luxury cars. So, as soon as I was in a position to purchase one, I did. In certain industries you only have one time to make the initial impression that allows you to stay in the graces of the movers and shakers. Movers and shakers are looking for a certain level when it comes to people with whom they deal.

When I began driving luxury, I noticed a night and day difference in how people responded to me. Many who were skeptical of the effectiveness of me as a motivational speaker in my mid-twenties seemed to magically lose the ideologies when they saw the emblem on my hood. People who were hesitant to do business with me all of a sudden were breaking their necks to do business when I stepped into the game projecting the level on which I saw myself and exhibiting the characteristics of people who were already there.

These are not made up ideologies; all of this is from real-life experiences. This is the world we live in, so although you are full of brilliance, genius, and talent the outward reflection of the level you've set for yourself will get you into doors that aren't readily available to those who don't project an image of belonging. Know your dream's image, spirit, and swagger, and play the game effectively.

So What Now?

After you've made your entrance properly into the arena of your dream, you can rest assured that you've created comfort in the minds of people in your industry and they are more receptive and willing to deal with you. Remember that all of this "up front" emphasis is stated because you need to get to a place where people are receptive to the gifts and talents that you possess.

There's no point in being talented in an area and not exhibiting the outward savvy of someone who belongs in your area and level of talent.

You can create by nature, but people are the doors you must go through to get to your ultimate destination. This is meant to create more than just a fighting chance for you to enter the realm of your dream. Creating your dreams is not an easy feat, so any advantage you can create for yourself, especially visual, creates an advantage. My purpose in this is to help you get people's minds receptive enough to the point that there are the least amount of mental barriers present when you unveil your talents and genius. The bottom line is that the more comfortable you can make people by appealing to their visual nature, the better chance you have of them being receptive to your gifts and talents. It positions you to have any particular person help you to go further in whatever you do or create.

There's No Room for Humility in the Sale

You have to believe in yourself and sell your creation. Your belief is what ultimately sells your creation. Whether it's "selling" in the literal or figurative sense of the word, people must be sold on you and what you bring to the table. The motivational legend George C.

Fraser says, "Two things are constant at all times: people are buying and selling." You can be driving at 4:00 a.m. and see an advertisement for McDonald's on a billboard, and it will convince you that you are hungry even if you aren't.

The previous section shows how to make an effective entrance into any arena, but the purpose of this entrance is to sell people on your gifts and talents because people hold the keys to many doors. I don't know about you, but our Creator has never zapped me anywhere. I've never been telepathically transported to a radio interview, book signing, or television set. Someone was sold on me enough to open the door for me to be in these places. Because of the degree of how deep I've gotten into my profession, I find myself in front of many audiences with people twice my age. On cue after I speak, someone will tell me that I initially looked the part, but when I opened my mouth the person knew I was for real.

This is not a braggadocio's statement, rather one of absolute truth. My outward appearance quieted some of the initial skepticism that an age gap can incur, but my essence shining through my words is what ultimately gave me favor with the person who stands in front of me at every speech. I want to give you favor among men and help you play the game effectively enough to where the hearts of men are ready and willing to receive whatever it is you have to deposit. God created us all to make spiritual impartations with our creations, but understanding the nature of man will allow you to do this with more effectiveness.

There's never room for humility in any sale—just make sure you deliver!

The right outward appearance makes a hard pitch before saying one word out of your mouth. But delivering is what takes you over the top. Believe in yourself and never shrink to accommodate others. People admire the courage to sell yourself and your creation with audacity. Confidence is a trait most people lack, so they'll admire it in you. Try not to be brash or arrogant when selling yourself, but understand the message that confidence conveys.

Confidence is an intriguing trait and makes people want to know and see more.

Once you are allowed to enter the room and you deliver, there are no bounds to your possibilities. People will see the truth of your talents, abilities, and creations, because all truth is spiritually derived and impacts those who encounter it.

All of this is natural positioning to make a spiritual impact. Find your dream, vision, and creation in these words and create accordingly. Remember that you have face-to-face encounters with people, so understand their nature and create accordingly. You have the power go into the arena of your dream or make an entrance. These are the keys to do so. Exhibit the allure and the swagger of your dream, deliver once you get into the door, and experience the unlimited bounds of uncommon success.

The Outward Appearance and Success

I wish I could change the rules
But this is the society in which we reside
So observing its inner workings
Reveals rules by which we must abide

It's the "up front" game
That governs our society
But playing the game effectively
You'll never enter a room quietly

When people are sold
Without you saying a word
And you actually deliver
An explosion in their minds you have incurred

With preconceived notions removed
And opinions they premeditate
Existing questions and fears
Yes, you did alleviate

When your swagger spoke
Of those who successfully fit the bill
They see your look just opened the door
As your genius attests to God's perfect will

Yes, you've made an impact
With that thing only you can do
But if you neglected the outward
Would they have ever had a clue

That such genius, brilliance, and greatness
Existed in the form of you
But to their sensory elements
You were so keenly attuned

And yes, please do remember
There's no room for humility in any sale
As your first impression should impact to a place
Which cannot be measured by scale

—Matthew C. Horne

Notes and Insights

Chapter 7: Something Has to Give

"Sometimes you have to turn water to wine until you get your own distillery." —Matthew C. Horne

Every dream, desire, and deep yearning to create is in no way a co-incidence. The blueprints of you naturally show up in these forms. You cannot become something of which you are not aware, so destiny assists us in understanding ourselves and what we showed up to create through these forms of divine communication.

"The way" to achieve your dreams, as discussed earlier in the book, is real. It's a concern that keeps many from even entertaining the possibility of creating whatever is missing in their lives. But people who operate in their creative essence are often rewarded, even if it's not the reward they figured would await when it's all said and done.

We, as human beings, are the vehicles of creation. Having power and dominion in this realm places the creation of anything on the earth squarely in our hands. Never be discouraged in the creation process, because you have an endless creative capacity. Failure is only final when you accept the reality of it as being final. We will all make mistakes during our journey, but our power is found in the ability to take corrective measures.

Even if you fail in the process of creating, there's always a drawing board to readjust and revise your strategy. The most prominent sports have half-time, which is a period midway through the game that allows each team to readjust and revise their strategies mid-game. Corporations have staff and board meetings for this same purpose. High achievers are no stranger to the drawing board because it keeps their creative strategy sharp and allows them to maximize creative potential.

Create Until It's the Way You Envisioned It

Honestly speaking, when it comes to creating it could be door number 1, 2, 3, 4, or 5. People rarely ever get it right the first go round. Many parents say that they became better parents with each additional child, because they learned things from parenting each previous child that sharpened their parental skills and gave them more parental acumen.

If something doesn't turn out the way you want it, simply consult your drawing board.

It's a courageous feat to create anything in this life; it's even more courageous to continue to create when things don't go your way.

Repeatedly choosing to create and not receiving the outcome you envisioned is a truly disheartening thing. There were and still are times in my career that prove to be difficult, as things don't always go as planned. It can drive you to a point where you even question God and His reasoning for pursuing the creation of the gifts that clearly came from Him.

In a time like this, I actually did question God. I didn't understand why something I put my complete being into did not work out as I had planned it. You may find yourself barely surviving in the midst of the creation of your dreams and desires and be tempted to turn back, as I have felt in many situations. But one day I received a revelation that changed my mindset forever. If we have an endless creative capacity, this means that we can create our way out of any situation.

This means that finalities are a manmade illusion of the mind when we have the power to change any situation resulting from our creative essence.

Instead of focusing on the reality surrounding situations that hadn't gone my way, I chose to focus on creating my way out, as opposed to dwelling on the reality of it.

Every problem has a solution, and focusing on the solution will naturally bring you to a place where you're consciously focused on creating it.

Your Creator does not leave you out to dry. If you stay in the game long enough, something has to give. Another realization I've stumbled upon recently is that we can work as hard as we possibly can at creating anything as human beings but ultimately we need a "break" for our creations to thrive. "Breaks" are supernatural, but your willingness to create the unseen vision and dream is a supernatural act, as you are attempting to bring about something you cannot tangibly see.

When you choose to create, you automatically place yourself in a supernatural state and are privileged to experience the flow and orchestration of the supernatural. Ultimately, something will give. Whether it's a chance encounter or just being in the right place at the right time, something will ultimately give and allow your creation to thrive.

Signs and Markers

Even if things don't go the way you initially planned in your dream pursuits and creative endeavors, observe the reality that surrounds you. Often you'll see that there are clear signs and markers that you are moving in the right direction. These signs and markers are usually accompanied by a sustaining grace that somehow keeps you afloat throughout the roughest periods in a creative season. Be still and breathe when you encounter a rough patch and see the grace that surrounds you. When you observe the signs and markers and sustaining grace you'll see your Creator and know you are on the path to a breakthrough.

The Process

Although destiny shows itself in spiritual desires and supernatural clarity, there is a process to arriving at this place.

The stage has a funny way of appearing when you can grace it without falling off of it.

Even though you clearly have a destiny and it speaks to you with regularity, there is still a process reflected in your personal evolution that you must complete before you can grace the stage.

Most people fear adversity, but it is one of the greatest allies to someone who takes steps to fulfill their destiny.

Adversity was never meant to break you, rather to create breakthroughs.

Adversity has a way of introducing us to facets of ourselves we never knew existed. Adversity has a way of raising our awareness of ourselves and everything around us, which has relevance to our dreams and creations. So, trust that the stage will appear when the process of evolution has completed itself to a degree that your awareness matches the dreams and creations in you.

The Formula for Creation

In this last section of the chapter I'd like to clearly articulate the formula for how to create anything that's missing with the urgency of NOW. The three creative elements of faith, energy, and intention will allow you to create virtually anything.

Faith

The creative person always has the element of faith present, regardless of their intended creation.

Faith is the ability to see beyond any reality that surrounds the things you aspire to create and focusing solely on the possibility of it happening.

Faith is your first-class ticket into the limitless and the cornerstone of all significant creation, past, present, and future. Faith is your pass into the supernatural flow of creation, because creation is supernatural. It's the belief in what's not tangible in the natural, so if you have faith, you have access to a different set of laws than what you see on a daily basis governs this world.

In the world, what you see is what you get. In the supernatural, what you don't see is what you get. The realm that you respect is the provision you will experience.

These words are renewed daily because every morning we have a choice as to what realm will govern our thinking, thus affecting our choice and creating our reality. Create a supernatural reality by pursuing whatever is missing and experience the reality of a supernatural life with supernatural provisions.

Energy

Energy is an important creative resource. Whatever you place your energy into you create. Your energy flows to the reality that you respect. If you have a desire that's beyond what you see and you choose to not take the faith approach by dwelling on the reality around you, your energy will go there as well. Your energy will go into staying average. What I mean by "average" is not pursuing the burning desire of NOW that speaks to you and urges you to enter a higher plain of existence and evolution. Faith takes you from the realm of average and allows you entrance into the limitless realm of infinite possibilities. There are no limits in the supernatural, as there are no limits to you. But given the reality that we have choice, this suggests that we have to place our energy into creating the faith desires we've chosen to entertain by taking natural steps towards a supernatural end.

When you choose the route of faith and do away with contrary realities to the burning desire of NOW, you will place your energy into the creation of this desire because you believe it's possible regardless of the reality that natural indicators may not be present. When your faith and your energy are immersed into the creation of anything, you've placed your being into the creation of it. When your being is placed into the creation of anything, it will occur. Something will give because you are too aligned spiritually in laws of creation for an act of creation not to take place.

As human beings, our beings must be encompassed in the creation process. God is uninhibited spiritual energy, but we have His essence coupled with a natural component. When we can tap into our spiritual essence and take the natural component of ourselves and align it spiritually through giving our spiritual pictures of destiny our energy, then we will experience a breakthrough like nothing we've ever experienced.

To place your being into anything is to surrender to the limitless flow of the spirit where all significant creation begins and ends.

Intention

Intention is the last of these creative elements. Intention is the ability to not look to the right or the left until whatever is missing has manifested itself. Creation is such an uncommon feat that it requires you to figuratively be dead to everything around you in a sense. It takes uncommon focus to create, so your eyes must be fixated on the prize of creation in order to reach your mark. Place your intention only on things that accommodate the creation of whatever you intend to create. Focus on positive messages and everything else that exudes a message possibility when it comes to your intended creation. Remain fixated on the task of the hour and discipline yourself to do away with anything that is detrimental to you remaining in a creative state. Weigh every decision you make against the reality of it taking you closer or further from creating whatever is missing, and you will soon stand eye-to-eye with your creation. Do this and yes, something has to give.

Something Has to Give

Yes, this road gets desolate
When choosing to create
But the necessary breakthrough
Will aid what you create

No matter what your efforts
They will all be purely in vain
If supernatural orchestration
Does not bring the moment that is ordained

The moment that redefines
And makes sense of it all
At times you may have struggled
But managed to avoid the fall

The universe sustained you
Because you created from your truth
But needed to complete the process
As adults do from their youth

And if the times get rough
Observe the perfection that surrounds
Understanding that you've submitted to a force
That inherently knows no bounds

In the unseen
Is where we all were meant to reside
And your moment of perfection
You'll see universal forces collide

As this collision
Creates the explosion of you
Yes, something had to give
To aid you in living your undeniable truth

—Matthew C. Horne

Notes and Insights

Notes and Insights

Chapter 8: Your Evolving Definition

"There's too much destiny and greatness interwoven into the fabric of who you are to believe that you showed up here to do and be just one thing. Evolve." —Matthew C. Horne

In playing basketball at the highest possible level I could have played at in college, Division I, a consistent question I was asked upon my graduation was: "Weren't you devastated when you didn't go to the NBA?" This is a question I was asked at every turn, even though I played at a smaller Division I school. Given the stage I played on, it could have very well happened. There's a player I played against who came from a small Division I school in the Carolinas who's now one of leading scorers in the NBA, so I feel where these people are coming from when I was asked this question repeatedly.

I was nowhere close to devastated, so I had to examine why this was. Many athletes playing at such a high level in college never seem to recover when things don't go as they envisioned. This also applies to people in general when things don't quite pan out how they'd like. So, my question to myself was: how did I make such a smooth transition from playing basketball on an elite stage to writing books and speaking, all without breaking stride? The still, small voice responded and said that I never identified myself as a basketball player; even though it was a burning passion of mine, it's what I did, not who I was.

Life is subject to change without your approval, and the only constant that life gives us is change. To identify with something in essence is to set yourself up for disappointment. I understand why many athletes never make it past the one defining characteristic of being an athlete. You've been groomed to play a particular sport for a large portion of your life, and obviously you have an elite level of talent to progress from level to level and ultimately grace the highest stage. But what the athlete and many other people in life through their various endeavors are not prepared for is when this thing ultimately comes to an end.

Everything in life must culminate, or else the various instances of genesis along this life's journey could not be established.

Everything in life that you do is what you do and not who you are. To identify with anything is to veil the essence of change within you. There was never meant to be one concrete definition of who we are in this life. That's why the phrase, "Freedom from the failures of the past and from the fears of tomorrow can be found in the realization that all we have is NOW," has relevance.

The Reality of NOW

The reality of NOW is that identifying with a season that has passed is borrowing time from the season that is set before you.

"Now" always has its own infinite possibilities and opportunities all in the same. Your Creator wants nothing more for you than to be the creator you were created to be.

In every waking moment there is a NOW that calls your name. Its voice has clarity when the noise of the failures of the past and fears of tomorrow is silenced by the realization that All We Have is NOW.

Many people won't detach themselves from their past because they fear the loss of control that pursuing the desire of NOW removes. NOW always involves a risk because it's new territory. The past, even if it has passed you by, still has an element of familiarity and control, making it feel like safe territory. The reality is that if you aren't creating something that is beyond you, you are choosing to regress and not evolve. Life gives us many constants, but here is one which is appropriate to this situation of NOW. You're either going forward or backward at all times in your life's progression; stagnation is an illusion.

Choose to move and create forward, as this is an ally to your evolution and freedom from the chains of the past.

The Truth about Pressure

If you aren't feeling the pressure when creating, you must ask your-self: am I creating from my ordinary self or my extraordinary self?

Pressure is a welcome commodity in the life of any high achiever. The high achiever understands that successes and failures of the past are just that, and that the real opportunity lies in the moment that is set before them.

Pressure is validation that you're moving in the right direction. Yes, the average person eludes it like the boxer Floyd Mayweather does his opponent's punches, but I hope you didn't pick up this book to learn how to remain average.

Doubt and pressure are natural emotions when stepping out-side of the box of comfort. The times of life's genesis will have this because it's completely foreign terrain, but that's where your true self is at any given moment in time—in unknown territory.

If we are created with an ever evolving nature and never meant to live a life with definitions, what else would our purpose be but to evolve?

The Purpose of Life

The purpose of life was never to live with boundaries and limita-tions. Choosing to accept anything as an identity is doing just that: placing boundaries and limitations on yourself and negating the opportunity of NOW that stares each and every one of us in the face. Identifying with anything reflects a sense of arrival. As long as no identity is present, evolution can take its natural course in our lives because no definitions are present to cloud the opportunity of NOW and inhibit the complementary flow of creative energy.

If you truly would like a glimpse into your Creator's original intent for your life, observe nature. Nature does not possess an ego, which is an acronym for edging God out. I believe that we are privileged to observe nature because it is a direct reflection of how we were intended to go about living our lives. Nature has no natural voice or barrier that disconnects it from the flow of creation. Nature has one instruction: to evolve and to thrive.

The one constant that is found in nature is change with the various seasons, which equates to evolution. What if we learned to change with our various seasons? What if the urgency of NOW was the voice that we acknowledged and we did away with contrary noise? What if we connected with the voice and essence of our Creator, which encourages us to evolve and change without ceasing? If we learned to do these things, our lives could be as peaceful and still as the nature that surrounds us.

Evolution is a conscious choice. Nature cannot be subjected to anything else but the voice and instructions of its Creator to thrive. Considering that we as human beings are the only species with the conscious ability to make choices, living in the ebb and flow of nature is readily available to us if we choose to experience it by heeding the voice of our Creator through its instructions to evolve and thrive. If you give your true spiritual nature reign over your being, there is nothing you cannot accomplish, especially when the supernatural dreams and desires you were created to create have instructions to thrive.

Observe nature and reconnect to your originating essence. The truth of who you are can be found in the constants that nature provides you. These constants are absolute truth because they emanate from the infallible flow of the spirit of all creation. Remember, the nature that surrounds us cannot choose; it is naturally subjected to the flow of creation and has no say in any matter. If you subject yourself to the same absolute truth that nature exhibits, you will subject yourself to the same effortless flow of creation that governs nature, thrive just as it does, and evolve into the originating intent that your Creator had in mind for you when He told over 400 million of your brothers and sisters to take a back seat to you at the moment of your conception.

Observing nature is a way to observe the originating intent that God had in mind for us when we were created.

Nature is a direct reflection of God because there are no interferences, thus allowing nature to be an extension of God in the earth in its purest form.

Whatever constants that are found in nature equate to absolute truth that cannot be negated resulting from their origin and purity. If we observe the absolute truths that nature provides and implement them into our lives, we are positioning ourselves to operate on the highest plain of consciousness available to us, quiet our ego, and live a life without limits.

These same truths that can be found in the nature that surrounds us can be found in the overwhelming essence and nature of who we are. Our only obligation in this lifetime is to bypass our ego and reconnect to this more pure way of existing by total subjection of ourselves to the originating spirit of creation and never questioning anything that arises in our spirits and subtly sways us to create it. Your spirit is the communication line between you and your Creator, so allowing this voice and nature to dominate your being is to remove any ceiling that has been imposed upon you and to live in the realm of the limitless, where you were intended to reside before creation.

The effortless flow of creation is at your disposal. Choose to create and not subject yourself to the failures and fears that surround any burning desire of NOW. Live in this most precious space that is set before you, and allow the spirit of creation to elevate you to places and heights you've never imagined. Believe.

Your Evolving Definition

Devastation is a choice
When life gives us many definitions
Observing the complexion of change
Will introduce you to new personal dimensions

How ironic is it
That change is the only true constant
So maximizing your potential
Is to allow change to be your compass

She will often whisper
With the voice of new desires
Leaning to your true nature to thrive
Embrace your new attire

As you see your definition change
They come and go as do the seasons
So to not identify with them
There lies a multitude of reasons

Yes, they will ask you too
How did you make such a smooth transition
When the urgency of NOW spoke
I acted, and chose not to just listen

There's too much brilliance, genius, and greatness
On the inside of you
To believe that one concrete definition
Could encompass your holistic truth

Nature is always speaking
Hoping you won't look to the right or the left
Observe her constants
And you'll find the path that is eternally set

Never set your feet in concrete
When you were created to transcend
The boundaries of definitions
Yes, change is the spirits trend

—Matthew C. Horne

Notes and Insights

Chapter 9: The Truth about Opinions

"An opinion is just a collection of thoughts in the mind of others; only you know your truth and are therefore obligated to live it." —Matthew C. Horne

To entertain a contrary opinion regarding what you believe you're able to create is to block the lens of clarity that you possess that sees into the realm of your limitless possibilities. Every significant milestone reached and accomplishment realized in my life has come at the expense of me not entertaining opinions that negated the visions from within I've always seen so clearly regarding my destiny.

The truth is that no one will ever see your visions and dreams as clearly as you do. This is a reality that the creator in you must realize and accept in order to reach your respective promised land, where visions become tangible realities. As you explore the underlying truths of personal triumph and accomplishment, the place from which these words are derived will become evident.

In reiterating the statement that personal stories in this book empower me to give you my most unadulterated glimpse into the inner workings of creative success, I will introduce brief life scenarios. These are experiences I lived, and they give me a clarity, passion, and power that create the most impact on you. This is my lens, and these are my findings.

I would like to explore some opinionated realities of how my first book came together. Let's explore some of the opinions that were introduced to me through people's corroded realities, mainly those closest to me: I was too young to begin writing a book of that stature and subject matter considering my age and life experience. No one knew who I was so the book wouldn't gain any notoriety. I was told to "get a job" while I was writing my book, which implies that I was simply dreaming and not creating something that could alter the course of people's lives and my own in the process.

I chose the words "corroded reality" because you are naturally endowed with the clearest picture concerning you. If I had accepted those opinions concerning my first book, I would have chosen to live in a corroded reality and been frustrated by the true reality that my spirit was nudging me to create.

You have the choice to live in the reality of truth, which evidences itself through spiritual intuitive urgings from spirit, or to live in a false, limited perspective of a negative opinion.

Don't Take It Personally

"Don't take what personally?" you might ask. When people relay negative opinions towards you and your pictures of destiny, often it's rooted in their own insecurities and the corroded lens they've imposed upon themselves. Strangely enough people are subconsciously rooting for you to accomplish your dreams and goals, and actually need you to do what they convey to you is not possible in order to create what's been missing in their lives.

I learned this through someone saying the words to me, "What makes you think you can write a book? I haven't even written one yet!" This same person found out my book had been released through a casual conversation with someone close to me and said the words to me: "You did it. Even in spite of all of the opposition, you did it." And almost immediately this person began to seek my guidance on how to write and release a book and shared visions and dreams of publishing with me.

Look at every person who poses any opposition to your visions in life as if they need you to succeed in order to give them permission to create what's been missing in their lives. Don't get caught up in what they say, because giving that energy will take away vital energy from your creative process. Just pivot and go about creating as you know you're supposed to do. Notice this person found out my book was released through a third party. I never felt the need to say, "Look at me," or "You said I couldn't do it, ha!" This is low energy that will undoubtedly keep you out of the flow of creation.

Creation needs a peaceful atmosphere to thrive, especially in the creative stage. When opposition comes, pull your best evasive moves and keep your energy focused on your intended end.

Some well meaning people don't share your clarity of vision, so in all actuality they believe they are doing you a favor by relaying these opinions to you. Let them believe whatever they want. Keep a good heart towards these people and continue to create as you were intended to do.

The success of your creation will speak at a volume anyone can interpret without you having to say a word.

Your freedom from negative emotions towards these kinds of people can be found in the reality that they aren't meant to see your visions as clearly as you do, so what else do you expect from someone given this truth? Be silent. Be still. Create.

The Truth of Reality

Realities are real concerning anything and will ultimately determine where you place your faith and creative energy. The reality that you respect is the reality that you create. All creation is entrenched in belief. Where your belief is placed dictates the quality of life you will experience.

Opinions carry with them the weight of reality. Realizing this makes it difficult to entertain an opinion that doesn't line up with who you know you are in your core. Usually negative opinions are the reality of how a person views you.

If you accept a negative opinion, you're choosing to accept a reality which is embodied by falsities that contradict the truth urging you to create.

Always choose the reality of possibility concerning the creations that nudge you to create them.

Entertaining the possibility of creating keeps your mind in a space of creation, which aligns itself to the actualization of your vision.

Once your being is consumed by the reality of you being able to create anything, look out because it's only a matter of time before you stand eye-to-eye with the tangible reality of your creation.

Creation's Two-Way Street

The universe is very balanced. Every urging you receive from spirit has a landing place for your creation, in people who are in need of what you were sent here to create. We are all interrelated in that we all creatively solve the needs of one another. Everything around you that serves you is ultimately someone's creation. Your creation will serve someone in the same capacity if you allow it to. Choose to create, and do it NOW.

All spiritually inspired creation has light as aforementioned. Light brings clarity and enlightenment to all who encounter it. That inner picture of destiny nudging you to create is someone's answer, believe it. People are waiting for you to do the right thing and entertain the right reality and create.

Imagine if I had accepted the negative opinions stemming back to my English professors who told me I wouldn't make it as an English major. Picture the impact that me believing I was too young to write books of this nature would have on you, the reader.

It is my belief that you have been enlightened in some way and maybe even have a clearer sense of yourself by this point in the book. Observe the reality that this was made possible by my willingness to entertain the right opinions and realities concerning my creation. Friends, we are more dependent on one another then you could imagine. People need you to bring the visions you possess from eternity into time to provide a blessing to all who encounter your creation.

Not only are people impacted by your creations, but you are as well. Remember, the universe is balanced, so what you make happen for others, through universal law, has to find its way back to you. Observe the example that most wealthy people are creators. The beautiful thing about operating in your creative genius is that there are no limits to what you can create, and your creation can take on a momentum all its own and redefine your life in many ways.

In this current recession, it becomes more and more evident that creators are positioning themselves to thrive. You would never lay yourself off! As a creator, you just fine tune things until they reach the place you know they should be. Truthfully speaking, if you research wealthy people, it's evident that they had the audacity to create the unseen and their reality changed drastically because of this.

One of my good friends says, "You're only one idea away." Truthfully speaking, we all have the same access to the unlimited field of spirit where these ideas originate. The idea has power when you find the audacity to entertain the possibility of creating it and allowing this reality to be your reality until it is your reality. What will you create?

Self-Reliance Is God-Reliance

Dr. Wayne Dyer says in his book, The Power of Intention, "Choosing to trust in yourself is choosing to trust in the same wisdom that created you." My interpretation of this statement is that when you subject yourself only to the belief that your Creator has concerning the abilities He's placed in you, you are choosing to create the reality that your Creator knows but you cannot tangibly see.

Self-reliance is God reliance in the regard that you have everything inside of you to become what you are uniquely created to be.

Success is one of the most intrinsic things that exists. It stems from a willingness to go inside of yourself and create what only you see. Self-reliance will always shield you from negative opinions because your reliance is placed squarely on the omniscient perspective of your Creator and the intended end He had in mind when He endowed you with your pictures of destiny. His only hope is that you would rely on this reality through Him and create as you were created to do.

Sidelined Voices

When you choose to create you're the one who's in the game. Very few people have the courage and audacity to attempt to bring something into the seen realm from the clear blue sky. Negative opinions are often people who chose the sidelines in life, who do nothing more than contemplate their dreams and desires and in many ways want you beside them.

What business do you have listening to someone who is on the sidelines when you're the one who's in the game?

Society's box is filled with voices of mediocrity. In observing life over the years, I've seen that people collectively would rather exist with a life of security in a close-knit box of predictability than enter the unknown waters where limitless ability is present. Subject your life to the voice of truth, which knows your beginning from your end.

Create your way out of society's box, and you'll realize that the sound you heard while inside was dirt being shoveled on top of it!

The Truth about Opinions

If an opinion is just a collection of thoughts
In the minds of others
Then why entertain
Foolish thoughts that are uttered

Only you know your truth
Evidenced in your unique lens
The unimaginable life is accessed to you
If heading the voice of spirit is your trend

Please do not take it personally
When they relay thoughts from their perspective
It's a necessary evil
Like major classes compared to an elective

But your heart's desire
Is what should always have true relevance
And the voice of truth within
Should always take precedence

To any contrary opinion
Yes, this is life mastery
When you are not deterred by negative words
Or the high praise of flattery

When the only thing that matters
Is the creation of your truth
Your internal joy and purity
Will rival that of adolescent youth

How else can they see it
If this was only bestowed to you
With an altogether different reality
How can they see it with the clarity you do

It's not their fault
So don't harbor negative feelings
But simply embrace the truth
That negative opinions are accompanied by ceilings

—Matthew C. Horne

Notes and Insights

Notes and Insights

Chapter 10: The Power of a Level

"No oe will ever respect your level until you first create it." —Matthew C. Horne

Earlier, I discussed "levels" and the important role they play with regard to anything you do in life. There are multiple levels present in everything that you aspire to do and achieve. This story displays how to establish your level and never be persuaded in any other direction once you do so.

In my senior year of high school, my ultimate goal was to play Division I basketball. I was honest with myself in assessing my talents and knew this was where I belonged. Throughout my senior season, I was recruited by schools on all levels of college basketball, including Division I, Division II, and Division III.

The Division II and Division III schools were showing the most interest even though my eventual college, Coastal Carolina University, let me know I was still on their radar. There comes a point in time after that senior season is over that a player begins to take visits to different colleges who have been recruiting him throughout the season. I was visiting mostly Division II schools, and every time I went on a recruiting visit something just wasn't right.

I knew in my heart of hearts that I was good enough to play Division I basketball, and I didn't want my mother to have to pay a dime for my education. Division I schools give full athletic scholarships to their basketball athletes. The Division II schools could not offer the same type of scholarships. They could give me a partial scholarship, but this is not what I believed my talents warranted, and truthfully speaking my level was established.

So I visited several schools and mid-May rolled around, which represents the deadline for the signing period. Colleges have limited time periods in which the National Collegiate Athletic Association allows them to sign athletes for various sports. The middle of May typically is the ending of the collegiate basketball signing period. The time was upon me, and the pressure began to mount.

I couldn't walk the hallways without my fellow students and school faculty asking me where I was going to college to play basketball. As the deadline was approaching, my coaches at the high school I was attending expressed to me that they didn't believe a Division I school was going to sign me, and that playing Division II was probably my best option considering that Division I schools weren't showing much interest as the signing deadline was approaching.

My mother, who was concerned with the financial aspects of college, was encouraging me to sign with a Division II school because at least they were offering me something. These are realities that rang true in those closest to me at this time, but ultimately I knew I would play Division I basketball regardless of how those closest to me saw it.

A level has no substance unless it is upheld at all costs.

The last day of the signing period, May 19, was staring me in the face. In my living room were two Division II letters of intent to play collegiate basketball for their universities. A letter of intent is what a university sends you to sign and return to them, which signals your acceptance of the athletic scholarship they've offered you. There I was with the deadline staring me in the face, and I decided that if I couldn't play Division I basketball I didn't want to play at all. Anything else was a compromise to me considering my established level.

May 20 rolls around, and I received a call from the head coach of Coastal Carolina University offering me a full athletic scholarship. I signed so late that I had to post date the letter of intent so that it was in accordance to NCAA signing period guidelines.

No one around me believed it would happen, but once again I had the clearest lens into what my heart was telling me would ultimately transpire. This could have never taken place unless I created and maintained my level at all costs.

Don't Fool Yourself

Your level should always be established according to the end-of-the-day-truth concerning your talents and abilities. I'm not in the business of showing people how to create fantasies. Reality will serve you if it is observed and assessed properly. Levels are always accompanied by signs and markers that you belong there. A Division I coach had consciously decided to recruit me after watching me play, and in essence let me know I belonged on that level. I observed players who played on that level and the characteristics they possessed and honestly weighed them against mine. In doing so I found many similarities. I also went on an unofficial recruiting visit to a Division I school and was allowed to play with the players at the university and assess myself side-by-side with the level I envisioned myself operating on.

> *Living fantasies serves you in no way. If you believe you belong on any level, go into that atmosphere and get a clear perspective.*

After playing on the team with the Division I ball players, I found out that I belonged. I also found out that I had a tremendous amount of work to do as well. Although I played well against them, I realized that they were bigger, faster, stronger, and very athletic. The contrast of high school basketball and Division I basketball was so shocking that I asked my mother to drop me off at a twenty-four-hour basketball gym at 4:00 a.m. on our ride back from this university.

People will attempt to impose many things on you based on their perceptions, even levels. Opinions are just the beginning of dealing with people's perceptions of you. It goes deeper into the realm of levels, which you must create and maintain at all costs. I'm confident that you can find yourself and all of your aspirations in the above story. My ability to create a realistic level was based on the fact I wasn't afraid to spy out the land by placing myself in basketball camps against the best players in the country.

All We Have Is Now

Lose the "small town hero" mentality, which creates a fogged per-ception of where you really are. Go to where the best are in your in-dustry, and stare yourself in the face and assess where you really are.

Be brutally honest with yourself because this will serve you in the end, trust me!

The Shortest Distance between Any Two Points

The shortest distance between any two points is brutal honesty. After you spy out the land and assess your findings, you're then ready to make an entrance into whatever room you believe suits you. It's difficult to make it to an intended end with no realistic beginning. In order to avoid living fantasies realistically, establish a beginning for yourself. Then the path to your intended end will be realistic, giving you a fighting chance of arriving there.

If there's anything that you want in life, always observe the end-of-the-day truth of your beginning and let that be your guiding force between you and the end you have in sight. These are two points of truth that match: a realistic beginning and an end that represents the vivid pictures of destiny you see. When you learn to allow the natural to angle you to the supernatural, explosions will take place in your life.

Having the faith to arrive at a destination does not mean there aren't natural courses of action that are vital for you reaching this place.

True visions are always supernatural in origin because they originate in the spiritual realm, which communicates with the spirit in you. A passage in the best-selling book of all time states, "Write the vision down and make it plain," exemplifying this statement. Yes, the vision is ever present because it ties directly into our evolution as human beings and moves us towards what we can't see, forcing us to expand our belief in ourselves and our Creator. This is evolution as it was intended to be: moving beyond the comforts of the seen realm and extending into the unseen through a belief that transcends what we see concerning ourselves and our Creator.

The above passage from the best-selling book of all time indicates that the vision cannot stand alone. A vision that is not written down exists purely in the realm of fantasy. A vision that is written down allows your natural mind to grasp the realities of a realistic start and intended end. Your spirit and mind will come in one accord to chart a path to your intended end when you establish a realistic beginning.

The "spaceship mentality" keeps many people in amusement park mode with their life. It's just days of fun mental getaways with no starting or ending point. Feel-good thoughts that will remain just that: thoughts! You will never be zapped anywhere. Your natural nature is real and cannot be neglected if you will create your visions in life. You will always have to take natural measures to reach your intended end, unless you have a spaceship boarding pass that guarantees you'll be zapped to the various destinations of life. Before you begin anything, learn to observe the end-of-the-day truth of where you are and merge it with the intended end that rings true in your spirit, and you will effectively join the two natures which comprise you.

Be Precise

My goal and mission is to for you to effectively create whatever is missing in your life, and do it NOW. In doing so, I want you to act with precision. Using the formula of observing the end-of-the-day truth of where you are and allowing that to chart a path to your intended end will allow you to live and act with precision. Most people in our society, because they are afraid to stare at the truth which stares at them, live stagnant average lives. The average person will wait for illusionary perfect weather conditions to begin the pursuit of their dreams and negate the opportunity of NOW that is synonymous with breathing.

Allow the end-of-the-day truth to serve you. Ask yourself the hard questions that many people bypass out fear of the answer.

The answers to life's hard questions are relevant to you arriving at your destiny.

The answers play a vital role in you reaching the various stations of truth that you must create in this journey. The end-of-the-day truth will allow you to live your truth. Don't be the year-after-year "I'm going to do this" person. Believe me, people who don't create a realistic start always fall into this category. I can make these statements because I've lived on both sides of this spectrum. Life is much easier when you establish a realistic beginning and create your way to your intended end. Which spectrum suits you best? How will you create it?

The Power of a Level

No one will ever respect your level
Until you first create it
So live your life conscious of this
To avoid living average and sedated

If you are governed by vision
Then of levels you must be aware
To gradually progress
And move up life's escalated stairs

Being honest with yourself
Serves you in many capacities
Being in tune with your true level
Will close the door to the realm of fantasy

As you live your unique truth
With parameters of reality
Then the amusement park mentality cannot exist
As truth gives it fatality

Living life with power
And with absolute precision
Begins with establishing levels
Which accompany your vision

Spy out the land
Before you make your entrance
To avoid feel-good mental getaways
Levels speak, and I hope you listen

Be truthful with your findings
They show you may or may not belong
Make the necessary adjustments in the moment
They should never be prolonged

If you know your level is accurate
Never be persuaded otherwise
And to those who never respected it
They'll respect your meteoric rise

—Matthew C. Horne

All We Have Is Now

Notes and Insights

Notes and Insights

Chapter 11: Creating a New Reality

"The reality that you respect is the reality that you create." —Matthew C. Horne

I recently had a conversation with a friend who told me she believed she was doomed to have bad relationships because her parents were divorced and have difficulty getting along. She believed since this was the main mental picture she had concerning relationships considering it took place at such close range, ultimately it would dictate her relationships and how they occur.

She also stated that this belief existed because none of her relationships with the opposite sex had gone as she envisioned up until this point in her life. In essence, the results of her thinking were staring her in the face. With all the reality of "bad relationships all around her" as the reality that she respected, naturally because she believed this to be her reality and fate, she was living it.

These words pained me, because I knew in my core that this did not have to be her reality if she chose not to accept it. I immediately brought a parallel reality from my life experiences to her to help her understand that nothing defines you unless you allow it to.

I grew up in a very loving household, but things were not always perfect, as is the case in many people's upbringings. My father battled drug addiction until I was six years old. I was no stranger to disputes between my parents growing up. My parents gave it what they could on and off until I was in college, but they ultimately divorced.

I used this example because in many ways my friend and I experienced parallel realities in our upbringing. I then asked her the question: statistically speaking, was I living a reality that would be expected considering the realities I was exposed to during the most influential years of my life? It didn't take her long to reply with "no." I said to ask herself, was it surprising that I came from a background like this? Would you, the reader, expect this to have been my upbringing with the reality of the NOW life I live as a motivational speaker in his twenties with a message of "possibility" and "self-actualization" that by the grace of God has spanned the globe?

I suggested to my friend, after painting this picture of parallel realities, that she had the same power to create her life and do it her way, independent of any definitions imposed upon her by life circumstances. The same power at my disposal that allowed me to create the reality of NOW is at her disposal, as well as yours.

What Reality Will You Create

I reached the destination of NOW because while it is true that I did witness these things during years in my life where circumstantial batter was mixed to make definitions concrete, I simply chose a different reality to believe in concerning who I was and what I wanted to create in the end. There are always simultaneous realities concerning any one thing. From the above example, I could have chosen to see myself as experiencing a life with drug addiction and destined for unstable relationships with the opposite sex. I can never act as if these things never happened around me, but I accept them for just that: things and events that took place around me in reality.

My friend also asked me, "Did the events of your upbringing ever influence your belief in what you would ultimately be?" I contemplated briefly and answered with "no." I always instinctively had a mindset of possibility of whatever I wanted to accomplish in life and never entertained a contrary reality other than the one I saw of me living my desires.

Anything that we want to create in life will always have simultaneous realities. One of the most empowering things in life is understanding this and choosing to entertain the possibility of living the reality of whatever you envision creating for yourself and dismissing all contrary realities.

Acknowledge every reality so you don't get caught in fantasy, but respect the reality of the possibility of you creating whatever is missing in your life.

The Respect Factor in Creation

With an endless creative capacity as human beings coupled with everyone on this planet being surrounded by the same realities, why do some manage to create what's missing and others don't? It boils down to the fact that the reality you respect is ultimately the one you will create. No one is without fear and the back of the mind thoughts of "Maybe this won't work," or "How in the world could I create such a thing when I've never truly ventured out?"

Given the fact that there are always simultaneous realities, it makes sense to only entertain the one that suits you best, positioning you to create it. This is another end-of-the-day strategy that is life changing and revolutionary.

> With all of the excess of realities that don't suit you present in your life, choose to focus on the realities that do suit the person your spirit sees vividly and constantly tells you is "you."

This shift in consciousness will be the beginning of the rest of your life, and undoubtedly allow you to create what's missing and do it NOW.

Create It ... and Do It NOW

Considering that we are Creator's before anything else and that it's the inescapable essence of who we are, there is no magic switch to negate this reality. The fact that you are creating at all times will never change. What you create will ultimately depend on the reality of what you deem as being possible. The reality that you are currently living is a direct reflection of what you see as being possible for yourself.

Destiny can show you clearly who you truly are, but ultimately needs your permission to manifest this image because you were chosen to create it.

It is to your highest benefit to believe whatever you want for yourself is possible, because this is the only thought that encourages you to create the reality of what only you see.

What has been missing from your life? If realistically speaking, All We Have is NOW, does it make sense to entertain the realities that are responsible for you not respecting the reality that will allow you to create whatever's been missing? Given our nature is to evolve, there is always something missing. This is not a negative statement; there is never a place of arrival so there naturally must always be a higher place of existence that we must create through respecting the reality of it.

There is only one person who can create your destiny images—you. What gives you the right to entertain any contrary reality other than you being able to create these things? Being endowed with an endless creative capacity places the need for perfect weather conditions to begin creating in the land of fantasy. NOW is your absolute moment. Any reality that challenges your ability to create whatever is missing is negated in the reality that there's only one you and only one way your pictures of destiny will enter the world—through you!

Peak Mental Conditioning

Do you know how easy life would be if when the urgency of NOW called your name to create the various things you've been chosen to create in this life and you only chose to respect the reality of the ability to create? This mindset delves into the realm of life mastery. This is peak mental conditioning because it uses your inescapable essence as a creator to serve you in the highest capacity and never live with any sort of limitations because you instinctively only respect the reality of possibility in all you do.

When we do anything consistently and long enough, it becomes our first line of thought and defense. The more you allow the possibility mindset to govern your thoughts and create in accordance with the best possible reality for any given thing, the more you will be unstoppable. Negative opinions that once rivaled end-of-days trumpets will be relegated to faint whispers when you adopt a reality conscious mindset.

Choosing the reality of possibility in everything you aspire to do will make unseen heights your regular stomping grounds.

At the end of the day, what other reality makes sense given your nature as a creator? The most self-defeating thing you can do is not enter the theater of possibility of whatever is missing in your life. Reality is real and will be with us as long as the earth remains, but your choice of reality will determine the indents you leave in the sands of the universe. What reality will you create?

Creating a New Reality

The reality that you respect
Is the reality that you create
Hover on life's pavement
Or reside in the limitless and levitate

Negate every reality
That doesn't suit your images
Each moment life gives us is precious
No walk-throughs, rehearsals or scrimmages

Our days are too short
And existence far too precious
To revere any reality
That challenges our desires progression

If All We Have Is Now
How can we compromise
The intended end that harasses us
Is accompanied by its prize

The grandeur of
Creating your own reality
Cannot be summarized by mere words
Or captured in totality

When you consciously choose to create
What only you see
On unseen heights you'll tread your feet
And live life at its epitome

You'll without question leave your mark
More aptly you will indent
With your legacy solidified
A testament to your Creator you will cement

It only makes sense
To choose the reality that suits you best
With so many contrary realities
In which one will you invest

—Matthew C. Horne

Notes and Insights

Notes and Insights

Chapter 12: Perfect Peace

"The only way to live a life of perfect peace is to trust God's perfection." —Matthew C. Horne

In my junior year of college I witnessed an event that borders on the realm of the miraculous. It took place at a time where I was questioning many things in my life and couldn't quite understand what my Creator's purpose was in me experiencing the things I was, with nothing in life going according to plan. I can say with confidence that my questions were answered, and my beliefs were forever changed with this one event.

I was playing in what would turn out to be the last game of my junior season against Liberty University. I wasn't sure whether it would be my last game because it was the second round of the conference tournament. The loser would be sent packing, while the winner advanced to play a game in the third round. The cycle continued with every team in my collegiate basketball conference participating in the conference tournament until one team stood alone and was crowned conference champion.

There was a particular player on my team named Brandon Newby, who entered the game having scored 972 points over his collegiate career, and he wasn't even aware of this. He needed to score 28 points to become fixated in the basketball record books for the ages. When a player scores a thousand points over his collegiate basketball career, it is looked at as an extraordinary feat. It takes a special player to amass this amount of points, and your university honors you by placing you in the athletic record books. Every time someone picks up a media guide after such an accomplishment, whoever scored a thousand points over their career will be mentioned.

Brandon hit shots during this game that I had never seen him hit, ever. Don't get me wrong, he was an extremely talented player, but he somehow went into another dimension on the court that night; it was poetic and divine. Every shot seemed to go in for him, no matter the difficulty. Basketball players call this "getting into the zone," and Mr. Newby was definitely there.

He started the game and ended it in the zone, never missing a beat. A knee injury late into the second half of play ended the game for Brandon, as teammates helped him to the bench. The applause for Brandon was roaring from his fellow teammates as well as the fans that traveled to watch us play that night.

After the game, the statistician alerted the media that Brandon scored 1,000 points for his career with his 28-point performance. The word traveled quickly as my teammates and I boarded the bus to travel back to school.

All We Have Is Now

A couple of days later Brandon came past my dorm room for a haircut. I was the unofficial team barber that every team has. As I was preparing my clippers I congratulated Brandon on such a legendary accomplishment. He then said the words to me I'll never forget, "That was God, Horne; that was God." I had to agree wholeheartedly, because God's perfection was the only logic in something this miraculous.

A Burden Lifted

It was a heavy burden to place all of my being into a game in which I saw no return in the way I fashioned it would take place. But I can say a significant portion of it was lifted after I observed the reality of what took place in the career of my teammate. I came to a realization that nothing is a coincidence and that God's perfection is always at work.

Dream pursuits are difficult. You don't always get what you put in. Questions do arise as to the purpose of it all. Less than ideal positions do occur at times that take you far left from your intended target, but in all that you do realize that God's perfection is always at work.

When you remove the word "coincidence" from your vocabulary, you'll learn to see God's perfection in all that you do.

Trusting God's perfection allows you to enter the realm where He dwells, peace. Peace is the creative space of the spirit. Creation needs a peaceful atmosphere to express itself through you. Cluttering your mind with worry inhibits the flow of creation in your life.

Most of the things we choose to worry about as human beings are out of our control anyway, so why worry?

We play an active role in the creation of things we've been sent here to create, but the determining factor always lies in God's ultimate perfection concerning your life.

Choosing to entertain God's perfection as opposed to the endless things life gives us to worry about is to live a life of perfect peace. Success and creation are spiritual entities that need peace to thrive. Every creation that lurks in your creative being will thrive when given an atmosphere of peace.

There are ways to create physical atmospheres of peace through various forms of solitude, but spiritual peace can only be created through the conscious choice to alleviate all worry through choosing to trust God's perfection.

Choose Peace

The purpose of me writing this book is to help you understand that every breath is indicative of the opportunity to create and to bring you to an awareness of the endless creative power you possess and to help you be the creator you innately are. My purpose is for you to create effectively and do it NOW.

This can be achieved through choosing peace. Your most significant creations will always have a spiritual origin. Where do you think the urgings to create come from? How are they accompanied by such vivid pictures? It's because your spirit, considering it is your origin and overwhelming essence, will always communicate clearly with you in this manner concerning what it knows you were created to create.

Staying in the flow of the spirit is vital in life, period, to accomplish the uncommon, but choosing to live a life as a creator calls for peace to be a part of you. Being clear headed keeps you in a spiritually receptive mode, as the spirit is the instruction manual to bringing things from "the clear blue" to "staring you in the face."

Avoid Conflict

Duality in nature ensures that conflict will arise, and in this instance I'm speaking internally. Your natures will always battle for position over you, and your choice decides the governing body of your being. Worry creates conflict with the creator in you because creation is such a spiritual process. Choose to trust God's perfection, and keep the flow of creation alive in all you create. Giving your energy to worry will create more worry, and placing your energy into the flow of creation will allow you uninhibited access to the unlimited, where all creation resides.

Everything involving understanding is enhanced by an internal atmosphere of peace.

The act of creation requires you to spiritually connect the dots until you manifest whatever is missing in your life.

It's nothing more than entering the realm of eternity through the spirit and extracting the pictures of you and creating what you see. Peace is your ally when doing this. Create what's missing and do it NOW.

Your Creator is epitomized by the words "alpha" and "omega," which translate to "beginning" and "end." To maximize our creative potential, it's important to take responsibility for the necessary measures that must be enacted to create anything. In the same breath we must learn to detach our worrisome self from giving energy to the outcome. The duality of this concept may be difficult to grasp because it requires you to take responsibility and create as if your inner pictures will never arrive here unless you do so, but also requires you to understand that some elements concerning creation are simply out of your hands. Choosing the spirit means working towards a clearly defined intended end and relinquishing all else, placing the particulars into the hands of the all-knowing Creator, keeping you in an atmosphere of endless peace and creation.

Yes, Brandon worked very hard to become a great basketball player at the collegiate level. But ultimately what took place in his final game could have only been scripted by an all-knowing Creator who specializes in interrupting the ordinary to deliver the extraordinary, which lets us know who's ultimately behind the wheel.

Live with the peace of exhausting all of your creative means concerning any picture of destiny you possess and understand that real magic is present at all times.

All We Have Is Now

Stand

When worry enters your mind, ask yourself: Do I really want responsibility for the outcome of things which I can't control, or is that better suited for a Creator who knows and sees my beginning from my end?

> *When you create, your only responsibility is to exhaust your creative means and offer the rest to God's ultimate perfection, where the script transcends anything our minds could fathom.*

I hope that Brandon's story helps you to understand that your Creator's reach is vast when compared to our limited perspective. The spirit is the most pure place that exists, so leaving the landing to God's perfection is choosing the limitless over the seen. Exhaust your creative means; stand out of the way and witness the power of eternal perfection. There is no end to the spirit, as there is no end to you. Choose the peace that comes with the reality of this statement and detach yourself from the things that eternal, all-knowing energy was meant to handle.

You have unlimited brilliance, genius, and greatness. Believe.

Perfect Peace

Living a life of perfect peace
Is to trust God's perfection
Leaving life's particulars
To the One who knew you from inception

Sometimes things make no sense at all
As situations don't go according to plan
Life begins with jumping from the ledge
Without worrying about the land

There's only one way to unveil
Your brilliance, genius, and greatness
By taking a chance on your destiny pictures
Avoiding the temptation to make them latent

People don't take risks
For the need to be in control
Needing every answer
Wanting a mental hold

That's a sure way to live
According to what you see
And negate your very essence
Which is in the realm of divinity

Where your Creator has intended
For us all to reside
There's no limit to the universe
And the ride will never subside

Emergence is nothing more
Than freely operating in new facets of you
But without taking the risk
To that genesis you won't have a clue

Peace is your ally
To the creator in you
Listen to the voice of spirit
And create as you were intended to do

—Matthew C. Horne

Notes and Insights

About the Author

Matthew C. Horne, motivational speaker and author, is the president of Optimum Success International, a speaking and publishing company located in the metropolitan Washington, D.C., area. He is an international authority on Maximizing Human Potential. Matthew is the author of *The Universe Is Inviting You In*, which is publicly endorsed by legendary motivational speaker Les Brown, and *All We Have Is NOW*. Growing up, Matthew's ultimate vision for his life was to play basketball in the NBA. He positioned himself to live this reality through obtaining a full athletic scholarship to play Division I basketball in college. Much to his surprise destiny revealed his true calling during his collegiate years, as he discovered a passion for motivational speaking. Matthew was told by his professors he would never make it as an English major, and much to the astonishment of everyone he not only obtained a Bachelor of Arts degree in English but was offered his first book contract before he graduated in his last semester of college.

Matthew's message is one of creating your own reality according to your vivid destiny pictures. Matthew empowers audiences live their unique truth, independent of the opinions of others. Matthew's message is quickly spanning the globe through his books, DVDs, audios, and motivational speeches. He is the co-host of the television show, *How to Survive in a Bad Economy*. He has also been featured on the legendary radio station WOL with his weekly minute motivational segments. Matthew is also a regular contributor to the Internet's leading motivational ezine, *Let's Talk Motivation*. Matthew will bring any event to life. Matthew is available for speeches, radio and television interviews, and book signings. All who encounter Matthew C. Horne will leave with a heightened awareness of their limitless possibilities and be positioned to live their Best Life Possible.

To learn more about Matthew C. Horne, please visit www.matthewchorne.com

Services

Motivational Speaking: Matthew C. Horne is the world's premier motivational speaker and leading authority in Maximizing Human Potential. His message has spanned the globe and will bring any audience to life through an awareness of their limitless possibilities and creative potential. Matthew is available for speeches, lectures, seminars, and radio and television interviews.

Testimonial:

Thank you very much for your recent motivational speech on "Peak Performance in the Workplace." I am very appreciative of what you delivered to our employees here at NASA Goddard Space Flight Center.

You brought your experience to the table and stressed teamwork. Your entire presentation was value-added. In a brief period of time, you stressed how employees can achieve peak performance by valuing their work and bringing their best work and attitude to everything they attempt.

—Michael P. Kelly
Chief, Institutional Support Office, NASA Goddard Space Flight Center

Also by Matthew C. Horne

Available at www.matthewchorne.com
$17.00 USD (ISBN: 978-0-9794550-0-1)

"The Universe is Inviting You In is a great tool on the road to your destiny. Each of us must choose our path and utilize the knowledge and wisdom that is guiding our journey from within, giving us the power to live our dreams." Les Brown (The Motivator)